WINGS

AS

EAGLES

WINGS

AS

EAGLES

*Thirty-one days of
prayerful meditation for
cultivating a deep
thirst for God*

Jabez Abraham

Paperback ISBN-13: 979-8-218-55993-9

Published by: Jabez Abraham | Desiring Revival Ministries

Turn us again, O God - Psalm 80:3

Contents

Introduction

Day 1: What is God like?
Day 2: Grasping the Eternal
Day 3: Infinity and the Constraints of Man
Day 4: The Possibilities of Grace
Day 5: The High View of God
Day 6: The Uncreated Being of the Triune God
Day 7: Who art Thou, Lord?
Day 8: Wrestling with God
Day 9: Awe and Worship
Day 10: The Emptying of Self

Day 11: Apprehending Christ thru the Eye of Faith
Day 12: What is Man?
Day 13: Woe is me, Beholding God
Day 14: Immortal, Invisible, the only Wise God
Day 15: Mount up with Wings as Eagles
Day 16: The Deepening
Day 17: Knowing God
Day 18: Pilgrims to the Eternal Kingdom
Day 19: The Goodness and Severity of God
Day 20: The 'O' of the Thirsty Soul

Day 21: Gird up now thy Loins
Day 22: The Eternal Word of the word
Day 23: Everything Stems from God's Nature
Day 24: The Burnings of God
Day 25: The Jealousy of God
Day 26: The God of Creation
Day 27: When Heaven Draws Near
Day 28: Dwelling place of God
Day 29: Entering into His Throne Room
Day 30: Be Still and Know
Day 31: Whosoever will may Come and Drink

Introduction

Why do we need another book about God? We have our
stories, television series, movies, books, blogs, and a myriad of
avenues where something related to God has been portrayed or is
constantly being communicated to us. After all, we grew up going
to Sunday School, learned the characters through the coloring
pages, heard sermon upon sermons, and enjoyed the great feats of
men and women of Scripture. But after all this saturation, are we at
a place where we have really encountered or desired to know God
in the way that our fathers have known Him? We look at the times
of the early church as people with no money, popularity,
technology, national support, and such, but still, we read of men
like the apostle Paul, who is considered in the secular world as one
of the greats of intellectual minds. We have Artificial Intelligence
(AI) and the Internet with access to millions of books and
manuscripts, yet we are unable to "turn the world upside down" as
the early church did with unlearned and illiterate fishermen, and
they reached the whole world with the gospel.

In Daniel, there is a bedrock statement that declares, "the
people that do know their God shall be strong, and do exploits."
- Dan. 11:32. Daniel wrote prophecies and visions, and scholars are
still trying to decipher what he wrote over 2500 years ago by the
inspiration of God. We can draw a line from Moses to Daniel, Paul
to Augustine, Jonathan Edwards to Watchman Nee, and others;
one theme defines them: they knew God. This knowledge of God is
not a Bible knowledge, nor is it the ability to interpret great truths,
but rather it is as the still waters that run deep, one who has plunged
into the unfathomable depth of God. This knowing is like what
Ezekiel experienced when he came to a place where, in progression,

the water was to his ankles, knees, and loins, in the end, he came to where the river could not be passed over, but it could carry him (Eze. 47:3-5). Knowing God is a lifelong journey; and the person who sits comfortably in his theological highchair and declares how much he knows God has not begun the journey yet.

To know God is to know life, to know Him is to fulfill all the longings of the human heart, to know Him is to know life eternal. Such knowing does not come easy, there are no shortcuts, but taxes the innermost being where one is content in silence to bask in His presence and enjoy Him. Jacob halted upon his thigh for the rest of his life to come to a point in his journey of knowing God. Our fulfillment in life is irrevocably connected to our fulfillment in God the Person. And it is our experimental attraction to God that will remove our attachment to earthly things. To Solomon, the conclusion of the whole matter was "Fear God, and keep his commandments" (Ecc. 12:13), to Micah, God's requirement of man was "to do justly, and to love mercy, and to walk humbly with thy God" (Mic. 6:8), to the elders of heaven, we are created for God and His pleasure (Rev. 4:11). The Westminster Shorter Catechism sums it up as "Man's chief end is to glorify God, and to enjoy him for ever."

This book is not a recipe to know God but a poor man's attempt to share the God he loves. It is a humble attempt to burst forth into words the leading of God and takes no personal credit for it. The words have no significance except that they desire to create a hunger and thirst that the reader may go to God on their knees and desire the One who is worthy of it all. To those who feel that they have wasted their lives and are close to the finish line with regrets for not seeking God, God still calls unto you. He can restore the years that the cankerworm has eaten and give beauty for ashes, the oil of joy for mourning, the garment of praise for the spirit of heaviness. Reading slowly in prayerful meditation can help the reader to still their hearts from the daily distractions that are vying for their attention. May God commune with you as you begin this journey of knowing God and rise above the noise and humdrum of society with wings as eagles. This is my prayer.

But they that wait upon the Lord shall renew their strength;
they shall mount up with wings as eagles; they shall
run, and not be weary; and they shall walk,
and not faint. - Isaiah 40:31

What is God like?

To whom then will ye liken me, or shall I be
equal? saith the Holy One. - Isaiah 40:25

The insatiable nature of man in his quest for something divine speaks of the residue of the Eternal, which has since been tainted by sin. In his eagerness to be like God, he made the ultimate folly of missing out on the greatest Being that he can commune with. When contemplating the Fall, the Puritan preacher John Howe said it reminded him of some of these great buildings in London, the country, or various Eastern countries where it was once a great palace or building but it's now fallen to ruins. At such a place, there may be a sign outside that says, "Centuries ago, such and such a king once dwelt here." About man, he said, "Written over man everywhere as the result of the Fall is this inscription, Here God once dwelt, He no longer dwells here."

God is not limited by time, matter, or space. He declared of Himself, "I AM THAT I AM" - Exo. 3:14, stating that He always was, is, and will be in eternity to come (Rev. 1:8). God is above Time and thus created time, His omniscient; He is above Matter and thus created the worlds and the heavenly bodies, His omnipotence; He is above Space and thus created and upholds all space in the Universe, His omnipresence. You cannot define God by His creation, for they are from what He did and not who He is. Man, on the other hand, is limited by time, matter, and space. The greatest of minds, as much as they would like to unhinge from these constraints, are still bound by them. Everything man does or thinks has been given to him. There is no originality in man but that which has been received. Even if there is a new dimension that man discovers, God is above that, for He would have created it for man to know of it. Wise Solomon said, "there is no new thing under the sun" - Ecc. 1:9. While there was no beginning with God, He always was, is, and will be. "In the beginning God created" (Gen. 1:1) speaks of the beginning of Time, Matter, and Space. While God cannot be explained in all His fulness He can be experienced in lowly hearts.

And so, we are back to the question of what God is like. While it can be a jest to the philosophers and the intellectual gangrenes of our day, but to the humble in heart who yearns after Him, God is the wellspring of life that quenches his thirst, the spring of beauty that never fades away, the nourishment that proves that "man shall not live by bread alone," the eternal joy which shall never run dry. The spontaneous response of a man captivated by His glory would proclaim with Habakkuk, "the Lord is in his holy temple: let all the earth keep silence before him." To the question, who then will ye liken me to, the echo rings from the eternal halls of truth saying, "there is none like unto thee, O Lord."

Prayer

O sovereign Lord, awful in majesty, thou who dwellest in the bliss of eternity, whose beauty inexplicably splendorous, whose power reaches through time and space. A most Holy God, whose angels are not pure in His sight. Grant us we pray a glimpse of thy beauty that we may worship thee in the beauty of holiness, as a dew which shares a glimpse of the infinite source from which it came.

Day 2

Grasping the Eternal

The Lord hath said that he would dwell in
the thick darkness. - 2 Chronicles 6:1

To embark on a journey, one plans a beginning and an end. When Abraham (as Abram) began his journey to follow the eternal God, he only knew of the beginning and not the end. Such a journey needs one's heart enlarged with the greatness of God and the magnitude of following Him in awe and reverential fear. To Abraham, God was big enough that he did not question the end but obeyed. It was not in God's best interest that Abraham followed Him. Instead, it was Abraham's best interest that he followed God. In the end, he did not receive an earthly inheritance but a promise, Isaac. In such obedience, Abraham was able to fall prostrate before God when he met Him at the tent door in the plains of Mamre (Gen. 18). God allowed him to draw near to intercede for the men of Sodom. Abraham had enough grasp upon the Almighty that he was able to contend for ten righteous.

God is unfathomable, He stands alone and is unexplainable. When we peer into God, there are areas where there is only darkness, and one cannot explain it no matter how hard he peers into the Holy One. There is an unknownness of God that reaches beyond human comprehension. We go no further but to that which the Spirit has revealed through the Scriptures. To be able to explain God is to create a god that we have made, an idol. The famous Chinese proverb that states, "A journey of a thousand miles begins with a single step," may give the impression of the ability of man to reach a destination. It is not so with God, for to grasp the Eternal, it must be sought with humble hearts and let God lead the way. When the Lord passed by before him, Moses made haste and bowed his head toward the earth and worshipped (Exo. 34:8). He let God dictate the terms and in joyful worship followed Him. Arrogance dictates that we should know everything when we like to have it, but that will never do with God.

To grasp the Eternal, we must bow down to the leadership of the Spirit of God, who can bring us to Mt. Sinai and hide us in the cleft of the rock while we see glimpses of His glory as He passes by. To these, the apostle Paul prays, "That Christ may dwell in your hearts by faith; that ye, being rooted and grounded in love, May be able to comprehend with all saints what is the breadth, and length, and depth, and height; And to know the love of Christ, which passeth knowledge, that ye might be filled with all the fulness of God." - Eph. 3:17-19.

Prayer

O gracious God, to whom belongeth eternity, we desire thee and thee alone, for our eyes are dulled with the dust of time. Grant us we pray a clear path forward to follow thee alone day by day, to desire thy ways above the ways of man and the allure of our fallen hearts. Let us see thy beauty, not pondering about our paths, but follow thee with hearts of love that have been lit from above. Grant us thy gift, the gift of love, to constantly abide by thy side, to walk close to thee. Then we, with rapturous voices, will worship thee and thee alone, to love, adore; reach thy shore with our faces unashamed shall we be.

Day 3

Infinity and the Constraints of Man

Behold even to the moon, and it shineth not; yea, the stars are not pure in his sight. How much less man, that is a worm? and the son of man, which is a worm? - Job 25:5-6

The nature of man is such that he must find the answer to all his questions in a reasonable way that satisfies him and ensures there is nothing hidden from him. Yet, man is extremely limited. He does not know what is going to happen tomorrow, does not know what is happening inside his own body, if there is an insidious disease that is waiting to be revealed, what is happening in the mind of an insect on the other side of the world let alone the vastness of space and their workings. Blaise Pascal, the great French mathematician and inventor, stated, "The supreme achievement of reason is to bring us to see that there is a limit to reason." Wiser words could not be stated better regarding one who tries to grasp the infinite God with the mind of a worm.

The worldly man with all his wisdom cannot find God, for the world by wisdom knew not God. Man has the concept of infinity but fails when confronted with the infinity of God who inhabiteth eternity. God declares, "For my thoughts are not your thoughts, neither are your ways my ways, saith the Lord. For as the heavens are higher than the earth, so are my ways higher than your ways, and my thoughts than your thoughts." - Isa. 55:8-9. The madness of those who think they can argue about God and speak lofty words against Him will on that day of judgment stand speechless in terror before the ineffable One whom they have spurned, unable to utter a word. Even the Psalmist staggered when he considered God's majesty in ruling the affairs of men, "Such knowledge is too wonderful for me; it is high, I cannot attain unto it." - Psa. 139:6. He acknowledged his limitation by stating, "Great is our Lord, and of great power: his understanding is infinite" - Psa.147:5.

The call to overcome our human limitations of the mind and see through the constraints requires a heart change to the man who has been made alive by the Spirit of God, where he has experienced God. This marks the start of developing a mind that can understand, though limited, the greatness of God. The touch of the Almighty in regeneration will remove the blinders that he is born with, and he begins to rise towards what he was meant to be: have communion with God. Having been made in the image of God, he can now enjoy the fellowship that was lost in Eden. Though we see darkly, we shall soon see face to face. O my soul, persevere until the Dayspring from on high visits thee, to be enlarged and rejoice in the greatness of God, with thyself content to be lost in Him.

Prayer

O merciful God, unto thee we come, our hearts dulled by the effects of sin, teach us, we pray, truths too wonderful for mortal man to bear, quicken us, O God, for in all thy truths lie life in purity divine. In stillness still, we desire to hear thee in solemn revere. Cause our hearts to be hushed, to see thy truth with the eye of faith, a truth divine for all to know, from a God who is true with eternal flows, may thy love be shed abroad in our darkened hearts as the sun that driveth away the night.

Day 4

The Possibilities of Grace

That in the ages to come he might shew the exceeding
riches of his grace in his kindness toward us through
Christ Jesus. For by grace are ye saved through faith; and that
not of yourselves: it is the gift of God: Not of works,
lest any man should boast. - Ephesians 2:7-9

In our generation, where promises mean little and truth has become the slave of convenience, we must realize that God always deals with absolutes. An abomination in the sight of God does not change with time, and the infinitude of God has in it the essence of an unchanging God. This is comforting to the believer, for they form the cradle of God's promises. The cliché acronym for GRACE, God's Riches At Christ's Expense, does not do proper justice to the nature of grace. Grace is not something conceptual. Instead, God fulfills His plan because of the channel of grace. Although God planned man's redemption before the foundation of the world, it was grace that brought it into the world. To invoke grace for our wrongdoing as an excuse is to violate what God requires of us. Grace and mercy are two very different ways that God deals with mankind, and they are not interchangeable. Grace is what God does irrespective of man's deserving. He makes it rain upon the righteous and the wicked, He sends Jonah to Nineveh and shows kindness to the wicked. We are told not to frustrate the grace of God (Gal. 2:21). Mercy is what we ask for when we see the danger and what God chooses to give that which we don't deserve. We rightly deserve the judgment of God. Instead, God chooses to show us mercy when we cry out to Him for mercy. While grace cannot be earned, mercy received spontaneously responds in good works.

To stop at regeneration as the end of our encounter with God is to miserably fall short of God's plan. The beginnings of God in justification or saved by grace (by grace ye are saved - Eph. 2:5) must continue in sanctification or being saved (And every man that hath this hope in him purifieth himself, even as he is pure - 1 John 3:3) and end in glorification (Receiving the end of your faith, even the salvation of your souls - 1 Pet. 1:9). The Samaritan who was healed of leprosy shows us a glimpse of how we ought to approach grace. He grasped the act of mercy, returned, and with a loud voice, glorified God and gave thanks, falling at the feet of Christ. His action was a direct response to the mercy he was shown.

To contemplate on the grace of God is to daily embrace the cross that God has for us to bear. It was grace that took Jesus to the Cross and mercy that pardoned the thief who knew his pollution when he saw the undefiled Son of God. True grace embraced loves His appearing and makes herself ready to meet Him. We see the grand declaration of the grace of God, which stands as a testimony towering over us and calls us to deny worldly lusts and to live soberly and righteously in this present world (Titus 2:11-12). A life worth living for and as an offering to God who is worthy of it all.

Prayer

Amazing grace, how can it be that Lord my God has died for me? Redeeming grace, no sweeter sound, of love that sought my soul. Not for me, O Lord, but for thee, let thy crown shine brightly beyond the brightness of the stars, for all eternity, the story told of love that won the misery of man. Can mortal tongue declare the praise of an eternal God? We plead with the angels and the hosts of heaven and lay prostrate at thy feet; to worship, to adore, to glorify thy name.

Day 5

The High View of God

In the year that king Uzziah died I saw also the Lord
sitting upon a throne, high and lifted up, and his
train filled the temple. - Isaiah 6:1

The loss of the proper view of God is the root of our troubles with the Almighty. To think that God is limited and that His power is subject to the world around us is appalling. The modern man seems to be in charge with his genius and ability to advance in the technological realm while delegating God to the "weak-minded" peasant who needs a crutch to live life. The stark declaration of Scriptures states that "The fool hath said in his heart, There is no God." - Psa. 14:1. The need is not for us to bring God to a high view but rather to lift our earthbound sight to gaze on Him, who is high and lifted up. It is not that God has changed. Instead, it is man who has chosen to scour the beggarly elements of this world in collecting refuse in exchange for the Pearl of heaven. The woman who bowed down and broke the alabaster box knew the preciousness of the One who was before her, while the high-strung Judas lifted his nose in pride and sealed his own fate.

We have flowery poems and sentimental statements of God needing man, and before long, we end up with the exaltation of man, though we would never call it that. Any generation that has lost sight of the holiness of God will immediately fall headlong by bringing the proper high view of God to his darkened, sinful, and fallen state. God on His throne sits in regal splendor; the seraphims cover their faces from looking at Him, in deep reverential fear, while covering their feet in modesty. The throne room at this very moment is filled with the sweet odours of the prayers of the saints. Worship is given where the elders and the four beasts fall before the throne on their faces and worship God (Rev. 7:11), and the four and twenty elders in worship cast their crowns before Him (Rev. 4:10). We see the fearful nature of our low and unworthy view of God that we are used to in our day when we compare it to heaven's response "the four beasts full of eyes within rest not day and night, saying, Holy, holy, holy, Lord God Almighty, which was, and is, and is to come" - Rev. 4:8.

We are in a terrible state of equating God just to the problems we face in this temporal abode, looking to Him as only a utility God. Our conception of God that is formed by the shallowness of our day will inevitably create a low view of God and turn our attention to an exalted view of self. This affects all walks of life, for everything rises or falls on our view of God. Isaiah's view of himself changed when he saw the proper view of God, who is high and lifted up. To break free from our shallow conception of God, we ought to search and tear down unworthy views of God, be it in our books, magazines, or leaders. Only when we repent from our folly of being satisfied with our convenient god of society will we be able to lift up our eyes and gaze on His majesty, which will bring us from this cursed view, heal the eyes of clay, and see once again to be able to climb to higher ground.

Prayer

Eternal God, eternal light, how dimmed are our earthly sights. We grovel in darkness with our fancied words while languishing in Earth's gloomy sorrows. Our hearts are turned against thee and dwell content in corruption. Turn us, O God, and cause our eyes to be cleansed, to be purified by a ray of light from thine bosom send. Embrace us by thy love and bring us to the joys of thy throne that we may behold thy beauty and worship thee alone.

Day 6

The Uncreated Being of the Triune God

He revealeth the deep and secret things: he
knoweth what is in the darkness, and the
light dwelleth with him. - Daniel 2:22

When confronted with something too great for man, the natural response is his denial of truth in its entirety. The existence of God is obvious by the fact that man fights so much against it. The reality of creation is made clear when we see the struggle of man trying to find meaning, in an uncanny way, to explain away the intricacies of life by embracing a theory (evolution) that is more like a fairy tale. In essence, man's impossibility becomes his opportunity to sear his conscience and deny the very truth that stares in his face. One God, the uncreated Being in three Persons in the Godhead, the same in substance, equal in power and glory. Athanasius, in 325 AD, when confronted with the question, "do you not know that at this moment the whole world is against you?" thundered in response, "Is the world against Athanasius? So be it. Then Athanasius is against the world!"

Words written by mortal man can get no closer to declaring the doctrine of the Trinity, such as penned in the Athanasius creed, "…we worship one God in Trinity, and Trinity in Unity; neither confounding the Persons, nor dividing the Essence. For there is one Person of the Father; another of the Son; and another of the Holy Ghost. But the Godhead of the Father, of the Son, and of the Holy Ghost, is all one; the Glory equal, the Majesty coeternal. Such as the Father is; such is the Son; and such is the Holy Ghost... So the Father is God; the Son is God; and the Holy Ghost is God. And yet they are not three Gods; but one God" and so forth. The plurality of the statements made by God in referring to Himself such as, "And God said, Let us make man in our image, after our likeness" - Gen. 1:26, speak to the similarity of statement from Christ when He declared His coeternal relation to His Father, where they condemned Him for blasphemy, for making Himself equal with God (John 5:18). He received worship as God when on Earth and eternally in heaven. John declares the eternal existence of Jesus as God from the beginning with "In the beginning was the Word, and the Word was with God, and the Word was God" - John 1:1.

To come to an understanding of eternal truths requires bended knees and softened hearts. There must come a point where reason surrenders at the altar of faith and lays itself down, being content to listen to the Almighty and lay a hand on its mouth to declare, "therefore have I uttered that I understood not; things too wonderful for me, which I knew not." - Job 42:3. Though there will come a point where human reason cannot support faith, true faith itself is not unreasonable. In coming to the Scriptures as a little child, one finds both faith and a God who rushes into the open heart, where all doubts flee, and God alone reigns and declares, "we will come unto him, and make our abode with him." - John 14:23.

Prayer

Unto thee O Lord, we lift up our hands. Our senses have been dulled and caused us to be restrained from beholding the majesty of thy glory. Declare unto us from thy place of rest in the heavens thy transcendent nature, O Triune God. Thou must hide us from our scarred reasonings so we may see thy glory and behold the Father, Son, and the Holy Ghost, the uncreated Being of God in three Persons.

Day 7

Who art Thou, Lord?

*Therefore let all the house of Israel know assuredly,
that God hath made the same Jesus, whom ye have
crucified, both Lord and Christ. - Acts 2:36*

Titles were of significance in ancient civilizations. The title of lordship was something that was meant to be given only to those allowed. For Jesus to be Lord was to incite sedition against the lords of Rome. Pilate washed his hands at the hearing of the Jews, who stated, "We have no king but Caesar." - John 19:15. It was a political move to get the submission of the Jews by giving over a "common man" named Jesus to be put to death, or so he thought. As per the church historian Eusebius, he committed suicide, sealing his own condemnation, and entered into perdition with bloodied hands.

To call Jesus as Lord was to deny the right of Ceasar to be lord. In today's technological society, man looks at Christ standing in Pilate's Hall, his harsh scrutiny, a pacifist and powerless, bloodies his hands by washing off the declaration of Christ, "I am the way, the truth, and the life: no man cometh unto the Father, but by me" - John 14:6. He takes pleasure in knowing he is in control. But the man on the Damascus road, who was one of the greatest intellectuals of any generation, the apostle Paul, when confronting Christ, paused in his assessment after saying "Who art thou?" It was the astonishment of a man who has been humbled, but the next identification of "Lord?" is equally consequential. It signifies the exaltation of Christ to the rightful place of being declared as Lord. The modern twist that one can receive Christ as Savior while living a life of rebellion and never coming under submission to the Lordship of Christ was unknown to that early church and is never warranted by the Scriptures. The Philippian jailer knew what it meant, being under the authority of Rome, when they declared, "Believe on the Lord Jesus Christ, and thou shalt be saved, and thy house" - Acts 16:31.

God declares, "I am the Lord: that is my name: and my glory will I not give to another" - Isaiah 42:8, which causes us to come to grips with the eternal Godhead and the glory revealed. Heart yearnings for God must be met with lowliness of hearts to be able to glimpse the greatness of His majesty. And when you are overwhelmed by the grandeur of the majesty of God and feel like your feet are faltering, take comfort that His love will not let thee go. While resting on Him, pursue after Him. Give God no rest until He comes, and in Him, you will find streams of living waters. The arrogant man will never find God; the hand that held the sword against Him must surrender the sword and all and lay prostrate before His blazing presence to be able to hear, "Rise up, my love, my fair one, and come away" - Song. 2:10.

Prayer

Sacred love, eternal life, crucified Savior, glorious King, Lord of all. O how we desire thy courts that are filled with the dew of heaven. Grant us this petition that we may behold thy beauty as we lay down our weapons and follow the Lamb. Thou hast sought us and saved us, thou alone. Deliver us from the coldness of heart, and may our love for thee grow day by day and not diminish with time. In embers of love, we feel thy warmth, in joyful surrender, we embrace thy rule over us. Come and conquer us, O King, for we are thine and thine alone.

Wrestling with God

for as a prince hast thou power with God and with
men, and hast prevailed. - Genesis 32:28

The struggle of man is something he is well familiar with. From the womb, he comes gasping when he takes his first breath, and soon, he finds out that life is not the rosy picture of happiness and frivolous fun but filled with strivings and learning from falling. In despair, Job declared, "Man that is born of a woman is of few days and full of trouble." - Job 14:1. There are innocent pleasures that men enjoy, and they are few and far between. The desire to know God is not something to be taken lightly, for wrestling speaks of struggling to comprehend, touching the Eternal with the hand of faith. With God, who is sovereign, His purpose will always be accomplished. But the goodness of God allows man to reason with the Almighty in order that He may share His own heart with the receiving heart. To the Pharisees, Jesus was a closed book, but to the disciples and the common peasant, their need was always met, and they went away full.

All God's gifts to his children are expensive. The child who does not know the worth of a diamond is restrained from handling it lest he toss it away as a cheap piece of glass. When the child becomes a man through striving, he is allowed to handle treasures that he values and protects. Such is the knowing of God, where it is through seasons of bareness, famine, and the crucible of suffering that those who plough through meet God and learn of Him. "I will not let thee go, except thou bless me" is not said casually as a nice-to-have option. Jacob was at the point of death where to let the Angel go was to die, but to cling to Him was to have his life spared. The prayer of Robert Murray McCheyne, "Lord, make me as holy as a pardoned sinner can be," must be said while clinging to the altar and desiring a life of holiness and striving with God. Strivings with groanings unutterable that take heaven by force. The crisis moments of men are opportunities for God to mold that man whom He has raised for such a time as this. We see that in the life of Rachel, who gave birth to the preserver of Israel, Joseph, when Rachel, who was barren, came to Jacob one day and said, "Give me children, or else I die" - Gen. 30:1.

Seek ye the Lord while He may be found, call ye upon Him while He is near (Isa. 55:6), still rings true. The causal seeker will never find Him, those who are willing to say "the world behind me, the cross before me, no turning back, no turning back" may set their face towards the ineffable One whose name is Holy. He is all the more lovely in His beauty, and in all things, He must have the preeminence. O that we may wrestle with God not shrinking about the cost of knowing God, for He is able to satisfy our soul as the wellspring of heaven that we might thirst no more.

Prayer

O God of heaven with whom is the breadth of man, we plead with thee to look upon us. Strive may we to seek His face, hidden though may be, in the similitude of looking at the clouds that hide the sun, until He shines forth. Yet in stillness, we worship thee, for there is none worthy. How soon we turn away and walk in sorrow, but what we see as hindrances to thee are graces, thy desire to see the hand that grasps the clefts of the rock and refuses to stop the upward way, to see at last thy beauty in full view. Grant us we pray for grace one more time that we might strive until we receive.

Day 9

Awe and Worship

O worship the Lord in the beauty of holiness:
fear before him, all the earth. - Psalm 96:9

The picture of worship is very much different as portrayed in the Scriptures from what we call as worship in our modern glib services. We are a people of checklist spirituality that gives little importance to waiting upon God. The trembling high priest who walked into the holy of holies had to carry a censer full of burning coals of fire from off the altar before the Lord, upon which he puts incense, where smoke fills the air and covers the mercy seat that is upon the testimony (Lev. 16:12-13). He was reminded that no man shall see His face and live, and the covering which hid the glory that came down brought awe and reverence into his innermost being. The casual worshipper who has been wooed by the many sights and sounds of this world has been made so numb that he has no sense of solemnness when entering a time of worship. Most of our "joy of the Lord" is nothing but the cheap imitation of working up the carnal man into happiness using any means possible. Such imitations may fool the street urchin but never satisfy the true worshipper of God who is clothed in humility with heart pangs for God.

The true beginning of worship begins when one sees the greatness of God in light of the smallness of himself and bows down in submission while prostrating himself in light of His majesty. This sense of humility can only come when we have a broken and contrite heart that overflows with love. When love is unrestrained, it becomes adoration, and adoration culminates into worship. The woman who came to the feet of Jesus loved much because she was forgiven much and worshipped Him in action by what she did. Another aspect of worship is sacrifice. Solomon, while dedicating the temple, sacrificed sheep and oxen which could not be numbered for the sheer amount of them, after which the temple was filled with smoke, so much so that the priests could not enter in to minister unto the people, for the glory of the Lord had filled the house of God. Sacrifice puts you in a position to receive God's abundance.

The thirsty soul can be filled in its longing after God when it begins the spontaneous heart response of love. This is not a sentimental or superficial love that condones sin. True love rejoices not in iniquity but rejoices in the truth (1 Cor. 13:6). Instead, this love, which is as strong as death, ascends with clean hands and a pure heart and finds its resting place in adoring the God he loves and in awe lays prostrate before His presence. Thus, in times of enraptured worship, time is forgotten, and one draws nigh to God to join the seraphims in the throne room to cry, Holy, holy, holy, is the Lord of hosts: the whole earth is full of His glory. From such enraptured worship, he comes from his closet in silence for having beholden such sacred scenes.

Prayer

We lay prostrate on the ground in worship and adoration, with our hearts stilled. In captivated silence, we desire to echo thoughts of God into our minds that are filled with chaos. We meditate on thy truth and glean treasures brought to life by thy Spirit and worship only thee. O wretched man whose pollution is the catalyst for Satan to hurl his fiery darts; depart, depart, let me alone that I may worship my Creator and my God. Let me see visions of God in untainted glory and stay there a while in raptured delight.

The Emptying of Self

*And the vessel that he made of clay was marred in the
hand of the potter: so he made it again another vessel,
as seemed good to the potter to make it. - Jeremiah 18:4*

There is a principle in the natural world that when a
vacuum is created in an area, it must be filled by something. When
nations drive out light, darkness sets in, when holiness is driven out,
perversions come in. In this downward trend, there is a point where
good is called evil, and evil is accepted as good. Our vessel, who we
are, that we hold as something grand, must be washed out, broken,
and crushed for God to begin preparing the vessel for His glory. We
know too much, and we can do everything without God. This
process of emptying is the first step on God's part to prepare the
vessel to commune with Him. God never occupies a heart that is
not prepared for Him, and we have to be "in the way" (Gen. 24:27)
to set our sails to receive the Beloved of heaven. "Behold, I stand at
the door, and knock: if any man hear my voice, and open the door,
I will come in to him, and will sup with him, and he with me" (Rev.
3:20) is just as much true today as it was then, given to those who
were "busy" for the Lord but full of themselves.

The process of being able to pursue God requires God to
break us, remake us, pour in, and pour forth unto others the
fragrance of heaven. Without such crushing of self, the petals would
never give out their fragrance, and the alabaster box remains shut.
A.W. Tozer stated, "It is doubtful whether God can bless a man

greatly until He has hurt him deeply." These days, man has little appetite for being stripped of everything he holds dear. The rich man came to the right Person but would not part with his idol of possessions and went away empty. In your seeking after God, this emptying is one of the most exhilarating experiences one can imagine. The hymn says it well, "Oh, to be saved from myself, dear Lord, Oh, to be lost in Thee, Oh, that it may be no more I, But Christ that [who] lives in me." To live in happy contentment, having no care or worry but living in the full light of His provision allotted for him.

Many imageries of such necessity have been given to us throughout the Scriptures. The three Hebrew children who were thrown into the fire were set free from the ropes that bound them before they met the pre-incarnate Christ, Job went through intense suffering before exclaiming, "I have heard of thee by the hearing of the ear: but now mine eye seeth thee" - Job 42:5, and so on show the need to be emptied before God comes. We read that no flesh should glory in His presence, and He will not share His glory with another (1 Cor. 1:29). Dear pilgrim, let not the daunting mountains that rise before thee hinder thee. He will be thy comfort and strength, and you will rise higher and higher and taste the Bread of heaven. Know thy God.

Prayer

Our Father, which art in heaven, hallowed be thy name. We come to thee, O Lord, desiring to be emptied of self and be filled with thy Spirit. We come knowing that the final enemy of man is "self." Plough deep into our innermost being and root out this hideous monster that lies within, hidden in secret. May we glean from thy word and be brought face to face with thee, having the end goal of enjoying our union with Christ and behold our God for all the world to see the greatness of our King.

Immortal, invisible, God only wise
Walter C. Smith

Immortal, invisible, God only wise,
in light inaccessible hid from our eyes,
most blessed, most glorious, the Ancient of Days,
Almighty, victorious, thy great name we praise.

Unresting, unhasting, and silent as light,
nor wanting, nor wasting, thou rulest in might;
thy justice like mountains high soaring above
thy clouds, which are fountains of goodness and love.

To all life thou givest, to both great and small;
in all life thou livest, the true life of all;
we blossom and flourish as leaves on the tree,
and wither and perish but naught changeth thee.

Great Father of glory, pure Father of light,
thine angels adore thee, all veiling their sight;
all praise we would render, O help us to see
'tis only the splendor of light hideth thee.

All laud we would render; O help us to see,
'tis only the splendour of light hideth thee;
and so let thy glory Almighty impart,
through Christ in the story, thy Christ to the heart.

public domain

Day 11

Apprehending Christ thru the Eye of Faith

These all died in faith, not having received the promises,
but having seen them afar off, and were persuaded of them,
and embraced them, and confessed that they were
strangers and pilgrims on the earth. - Hebrews 11:13

Faith is not the absence of facts; it is the eye to see the reality of the facts that are already there, that which does not contradict the word of God. "the substance of things hoped for, the evidence of things not seen" - Heb. 11:1. Thus, God's promise of a child that was promised through Elisha to the Shunammite was to be believed because of the greatness and trustworthiness of God. He never lies, and He is big enough to bring it to pass. Faith has substance which knows the evidence of what it hopes for. When God is the one who is to provide the evidence, then faith is the natural outcome because we believe God. The journey of faith began as a wavering walk for Abraham and was manifested in the self-preservation of calling Sarah, his wife, as his sister, but it culminated with the steadfast faith that was willing to lay down the life of his only son of promise, Isaac in full assurance that God was able to raise him from the dead. Thus, in Hebrews 11, all those whose faith is mentioned always follow with an action that proves it, and faith without works is dead.

This requires more than the natural faith that all of mankind has. The gift of saving faith goes beyond the natural and embraces the Person of whom is this faith, and our spontaneous response is to embrace Him and not just His teachings. Faith cometh to the receiving ear that is willing to obey God's truth, rejecting unbelief and made effectual by the Spirit of God. The greatness of the mustard seed is not in the size of the seed. Instead, it is the outcome of the greatness of the tree that it produces. Our reward in heaven is based on our apprehension of Christ through the eye of faith and the works that follow. To apprehend is to lay hold of or to make it one's own, and faith is enlarged when it knows the greatness of God. Thus, they were able to see the promise and seek a country not made with hands because they were persuaded about the Person who said it. Hence, the man of faith sees the promise given to him, is persuaded of the One who gave it that He is able to perform it, embraces it while not staggering at the greatness of the promise, and proves it by his actions (Heb. 11:13). We see it displayed by men such as Abraham for the promise of Isaac (Rom. 4:16-21), Peter walking on water (Mat. 14:28-29), and many others.

When Pilgrim ran from the City of Destruction, he was confronted by the cries of his wife and children, and he covered his ears and cried, "Life, life, eternal life." With the struggle of faith to apprehend comes our growing confidence in God's ability. The call of those who have gone before us is always to look unto Jesus, who is the author and finisher of our faith, and reach onto higher ground, going from faith to faith. Thus, without faith, it is impossible to please Him.

Prayer

Dear God, how limited we are by our unbelief. Our hearts are dull, and our eyelids heavy and unwilling to search out the deep things of God through the means of faith. Thou hast given us thy word that we may plunge deep and learn of thee. Hear us, O God, and cause our hearts to be enlarged, that we may by this grace shed the scales and rise above the heavens to meet thee and worship thee, with hearts captivated by thy beauty.

Day 12

What is Man?

*What is man, that thou art mindful of him? and the
son of man, that thou visitest him? - Psalm 8:4*

The famous Scottish poet Robert Burns of the 18th century stated, "Man's inhumanity to man makes countless thousands mourn!" This seems like a cruel outburst of a man in depression. Yet, the reality of such a statement can be seen all around us. The psalmist declared in awe, "What is man, that thou art mindful of him? and the son of man, that thou visitest him?" - Psa. 8:4. The query of the psalmist is a response to seeing, despite the depravity of man, the Eternal to take any interest in him. The greatness is not in man that God should come; instead, it is the greatness of God who even sought to look upon sinful man through the veil of His holiness. To save a wretch and call him His own. O sinner, flee from the wrath that is to come, is the cry of sacred Scripture.

The Scripture boldly states, "So God created man in his own image, in the image of God created he him; male and female created he them" - Gen. 1:27. Man was made for greater, and in his folly he chose to break off from life and go on his own, choosing death and decay. To the blood-bought child of God, man rises to greater heights than Eden. Now in his new position, he is joined as joint-heirs with Jesus Christ, partaking of heaven itself and seated in heavenly places. He has entered into a partnership with God as a co-laborer and bears the weight of bringing to birth the will of God that affects those around him. Thus, God chose to shut the womb of Hannah, for He needed a prophet for Israel, and she brought forth Samuel. The prophets were lonely men, but they did not get trained in the feathered beds of kings; instead, they stood on their knees in the harsh wilderness of Galilee and saw God shut heaven. They were hidden until their time of shewing forth, burned for God for six months, and sealed their testimony in blood.

Such is the need for men of our day to rise up and know God, willing to tread through dangers and towering peaks to reach heights where there are no crowds and the air is cleaner. These are men whose vision has been touched by God, and they are willing to stay on Mt. Sinai and are in no hurry while waiting upon God. Such men are the ones who are able to stand before kings and declare, "Thus saith the Lord Almighty." These are those who can shake kingdoms and bring terror into those who hear them. Thus, it was said of John Knox, who stood before Mary, the Catholic Queen of Scotts, said, "More than the armies of England, I fear the prayers of John Knox."

Prayer

Sin, the curse of man, the grief of the earth, the offspring of death. Who can peer into the abyss of sin, a cavern of darkness and misery? Woe is he who takes pleasure in it, for it is an unloving master. A thousand voices of sorrow in heart-rending cries with tears and shame found pleasure to dwell with man, to bring him to the bottomless grave. O, how can one flee the throngs of hell, for that will be your end. Flee, O sinner man, repent and fall on the mercy of God, lest all hope be lost at last, forever. Of such to those whom Christ hast redeemed, we praise thee, O God, for the greatness of thy mercy. We give thee glory.

Day 13

Woe is me, Beholding God

*Then said I, Woe is me! for I am undone; because I am a man
of unclean lips, and I dwell in the midst of a people of unclean lips:
for mine eyes have seen the King, the Lord of hosts. - Isaiah 6:5*

We live in a day and age where words have little meaning when dealing with things that are consequential. We ascribe greatness to something that may be as trivial as winning a game. The great need of our day is to reprogram our perspective when we speak of ascribing greatness to the One who is truly great. This is the One who has brought the world and space into existence just by speaking it. If we say there are trillions upon trillions of stars in a galaxy, and we have billions upon billions of galaxies, He is the one who calls them all by their names (Psa. 147:4). If we say that there are over eight billion people and hundreds of nations, to Him they are as a drop of a bucket and are counted as the small dust of the balance (Isa. 40:15). If we say that over seventy percent of Earth is covered in water, He has measured them in the hollow of His hand (Isa. 40:12).

When Isaiah encountered God, he uttered, "Woe is me! for I am undone," when Job, the most holy man, encountered God he uttered, "I abhor myself, and repent in dust and ashes," when Jacob encountered God he was afraid, and said, "How dreadful is this place! this is none other but the house of God, and this is the gate of heaven." To the faithful churchgoer, God is someone he respects and enjoys but goes home unchanged. To behold has the deeper meaning of absorbed gaze that has this experience of being made bare by the revelation of the most high God, almost a terror of the deep consciousness of self and the sinfulness of sin. When such a one has looked to Calvary and is cleansed by the blood of Christ, it has the heart-bursting flow of love and elevation of joy to new heights in worship and utterance that are too sacred to repeat. Unless one is made undone of their self-righteousness, they can never behold God as He is worthy of.

This cannot be worked up by the flesh. While emotion is involved, it is always a slave to truth. While truth affects the heart, emotion rises as a handmaid to heartfelt expression. While beholding God can help with sanctification, it must be guarded with jealousy lest sin hinders us and we are dulled into misery. Moses in that sacred place cried, "I beseech thee, shew me thy glory," and God was pleased to show enough to satisfy Moses and leave the mount with his face shining with the glory of God. In desiring God, we are brought low to prepare to receive God in all His beauty, where we behold Him and come from our secret place with faces lit with the light of heaven and hearts full of the goodness of God. The crystal drops from the snow peaks flow into the thirsty streams that lay low, which are ready to receive it. God is looking for lowly hearts that He can fill with Himself.

Prayer

Great God, whose name is holy and dwells in the light of eternity, come unto us and grace us with thyself. Oh, that thou wouldest rend the heavens and come down. Then may we see thee and behold thy beauty, a life changed and transformed. Hear us, O God, and cause thy face to shine upon us. Grant this day that we might desire such deep work of revelation in our hearts, though we come with fear and trembling, that we might, in truth, behold our God.

Day 14

Immortal, Invisible, the only Wise God

Now unto the King eternal, immortal, invisible, the only wise God,
be honour and glory for ever and ever. Amen. - 1 Timothy 1:17

The tragedy of man is that he was made for greatness. Personalities such as Beethoven, Vivaldi, Shakespeare, Michelangelo, Leonardo da Vinci, Isaac Newton, and others have produced masterpieces that stand as a testimony to the greatness of God imparted to mortal men in the beauty of the work that they produced through the mediums they conveyed it from, though tainted by sin. Though man was made for greatness while being subject to his Maker, yet he wallows in the misery of being a slave to sin. Oh, the tragedy of man. We see him in the gutters of life, running from one empty craving to another. He has been trying to reach higher ever since the Fall, to be like God. In his quest to rise to such heights, he has been looking in the wrong places. He has become dulled by the tragedy of life and sees it as a satirical joke. What seems elusive but attainable has been his endless goal, with each generation trying to outdo the previous. The immortality of man is that he has to meet God, who created him, and give an account after this life is over.

The invisible God declares His call to taste and see the goodness in Himself. And by faith, he can touch the unseen, by grace, he can know the immortal and be partaker of the wisdom of God. The worldly seek wisdom in the higher progress of education or philosophy, while God's call is to deny himself, take up his cross, and follow Him. The greatness of a man is not in his ability to conquer by war and destruction but in hearing the Almighty God who deals with man in a still, small voice. The response of Christ to Pilate on that consequential day where Pilate marveled that Christ uttered no answer speaks of greatness at its highest, power of the omnipotent God under control. The true man of God is heartbroken for the depravity of man who is content to grovel at the scraps, driven by his lusts, and die and enter eternal damnation.

The longing heart that sees the greatness of God and worships in humble adoration of this immortal, invisible, and only wise God is set free to rise to heights above as he kneels before this great God in adoration and worship. He is content to fall prostrate before his Maker and to enjoy moments of calm delight. To seek Him is the greatness of man, to know Him is the pinnacle of his achievements. The glory of man reaches great heights in music, art, science, technology, and such but falls terribly short of meeting the God of creation, who is the true source of what man enjoys in the first place. To walk with Him is the privilege of a multitude of saints, from the baker down the street to the man of learning who bows before Him with gifts of gold, frankincense, and myrrh. "But let him that glorieth glory in this, that he understandeth and knoweth me" - Jer. 9:24, is God's call to those who will hear and, with bended knees, gaze on His majesty and glory.

Prayer

Oh Lord, I lay in life's glory dead and stand in awe of thy greatness that thou desirest to share with man. O wretched man that denied the Almighty to live in misery, to fill his belly with husks of swine while wallowing in his own vomit. How I hate the sin that made thee our enemy. Deliver me, Oh God, to rise above the heavens and hate the garments that are polluted by the weariness of this world. Unshackle my vision to see visions of God instead of being content with the tragedies below.

Day 15

Mount up with Wings as Eagles

My soul, wait thou only upon God; for my
expectation is from him. - Psalm 62:5

There are moments in our lives that we come to where we find ourselves standing in the midst of greatness or something far beyond what we expected. It is a moment that is well remembered for a lifetime and something that causes us to yearn after, time and time again. It is a moment that is not shallow but something that deepens us and gives us purpose for living and the joy of knowing. It is a moment that one is hesitant to repeat and finds it too sacred to put words to and desires the contemplation of it rather than the explanation about it. Paul met such a man who was caught up into paradise (2 Cor. 12:1-4). Such is what God has in front of us to come to a place where we are told to wait upon the Lord with earnest expectation. The popular saying that the end justifies the means is not only invalid but also not true in the spiritual realm. The natural outflow of waiting upon God and desiring Him is the result that is portrayed as being lifted up with the imagery of wings as eagles.

To see the end of what it can be is helpful as long as we don't let that obscure the path we need to take to get there. It becomes a fanciful dream to desire the heights but not do anything to go through the depths of the valleys to reach those heights. Such is the nature of fostering a thirst for God, in going on with Him until the very end. Our daily awareness of these momentous times that God desires to bring us should motivate us not to give in to a life of ease and comfort. The soldier who is the most aware of his position is the one who is in the thick of the battle, has his senses sharpened, knows his end goal, and rushes to conquer the enemy. The strength for the journey is not in the calm and restful times of apathy but rather in the midst of the battle where the stakes are high and to become weary is death, and to faint is to surrender.

It was militant Christianity that saw the power of the Spirit manifested wherever they went, despising the easy life and declaring, "Must I be carried in flowery beds of ease while others fought through bloody seas," to the pulling down of strongholds and God glorified with communities transformed by the power of God. These are those who realized that our rest is in heaven and fought their way to win their prize. We resist Satan, the enemy of our souls, on the ground of the blood of Christ, for the victory has already been won by our King Jesus. The man who has an excuse will find ways to justify his position while admiring those saints of the past who shone the brightest. This is not a matter of ability or strength but rather the acknowledgment of one's weakness, where Christ's strength is made perfect. Go on, fellow soldier, seek after Him, wait upon Him, break up your fallow ground, and your mourning will be turned to joy.

Prayer

Let God arise, and His enemies be scattered, let them that hate the Lord flee before Him. O precious Father, I come before thee realizing my own weakness of flesh and blood which rises up against seeking after thee. The flesh within and the enemy without, the adversary Satan, remind me of the raging battle that is before me. Help me, dear Lord, as I put on the armor to fight the good fight of faith, to resist, to contend, and to die as a corn of wheat. May the glory be thine and my heart enlarged as I see my conquering King, the King of glory.

Day 16

The Deepening

That be far from thee to do after this manner, to slay the righteous with the wicked: and that the righteous should be as the wicked, that be far from thee: Shall not the Judge of all the earth do right? - Genesis 18:25

In the courts of heaven, we enter into sacred places that ring aloud through eternity of the works that flowed from the union of God with man. There are the vials of tears from the prayers of saints in bottles, there are the halls of faith of those who took heaven by storm, and then there are the sacred few who bore the burden of Gethsemane in intercessory prayer, which shook heaven and earth. The ingredients that make up such prayers are forged in well-tested anvils that have been touched by the fire of God. Those who have joined this glorious company have, in essence, partnered with Him to shape world events, such as John Hyde, Nash, Peggy Smith, and others. The Welsh intercessor Rees Howells used to say, "When you can carry a burden no longer, the Holy Spirit must take it."

This is not for the weak of heart, for such is the work that it requires strong backs that have been weathered through seasons of summer and winter to gain heights of trust from God. The faith that is trusted must first be tested and made sure before it is taken to the battlefield, and this takes time. There are no cheap imitations in God's armory, and the casual window shopper moves on, unable to afford them. He admires them and hopes he can buy them someday but ends his life in wishful thinking, unable to bring to birth that which is valuable in God's sight. The strong don't need the motivation of cheap imitations; instead, they set their eyes on their Savior and, in love, follow after Him, glad to be a bondslave in His service. They have seen Moses utter words of such weight (including the -- in his intercession), "Yet now, if thou wilt forgive their sin--; and if not, blot me, I pray thee, out of thy book which thou hast written." - Exo. 32:32, and the apostle Paul who prays with such earnestness, "For I could wish that myself were accursed from Christ for my brethren, my kinsmen according to the flesh" - Rom. 9:3. It should alarm us of how far our prayers lack fervency in seeking God. Knees that bear no marks of wrestling with God.

We cannot explain such depths of intercession without treading on holy ground. The picture of Abraham pleading with God for the city of Sodom gives us a glimpse of the magnitude of this work. An intercessor is someone who stands between the people who don't realize their danger and a holy God, knowing that justice and judgment must prevail. The classroom of intercessory prayer cannot be academically attained but must be wrought on the knees while being alone with God. The disciples did not come to Jesus and ask Him to teach them to preach or sing but rather to teach them to pray (Luke 11:1). To identify with the lost, though they may not see their need, to agonize for them, to enter into Christ's suffering, and prevailing until relief comes unto victory, these four stages are essential when God deepens our walk and expands our horizon where Earth becomes our battleground and God our Captain. Not all prayers reach God or are treated as equal by God.

Prayer

We come in humility, desiring of thee to teach us to pray. Dear God, search us if our prayer is for pretense or the praise of men and forgive us. Move us to brokenness and tears, which are thy treasured gifts, and cause our hearts to ponder on what's ahead with apprehension to make our calling sure for this noble task. Lest we be fainthearted and turn aside and bring sorrow to thy cause.

Day 17

Knowing God

*the people that do know their God shall be
strong, and do exploits. - Daniel 11:32*

To be able to begin this journey of comprehending God takes all of man. His intellect, mind, strength, and so on are tested to their limits when trying to desire God and continue this journey. Fostering a deep thirst for God does not come by chance or by shallow pretense. The con artist makes a profit by the effectiveness of his act to convince people to buy. With God, this process has intense consequences. To attain closeness, to be able to know God's heart and enquire of His desire for us. To walk away from such an encounter will be life-altering, where Paul, who was caught up to the third heaven, lived with a thorn in the flesh for the rest of his life. The gospel brings the good news that God reached down to mankind; the struggle of man to know God, who is now his Father, speaks of man reaching up to know this God who has so loved and saved him. And this is by grace as well, for our hearts are like coals in the winter, which need to be kept in the fire and stoked for the embers to continue burning. Abraham knew something of that when he chased away the fowls that came down upon the carcasses to defile the sacrifice (Gen. 15). God telling Moses to "let me alone" (Exo. 32:10), speaks to the intimate way that Moses knew God.

This matter of knowing God has, in essence, the picture of calm rest but also of deep contemplation and of sorrow. But this sorrow is something of what Jesus had when he was at the tomb of

Lazarus. Though He knew that He was going to raise him from the dead. He "groaned in the spirit, and was troubled" - John 11:33. This groaning from seeing what sin had done to mankind is part of our fellowship of His suffering that the apostle Paul talks about in that famous verse, "That I may know him" - Phil. 3:10. Those desirous of experiencing the power of His resurrection must be willing to go through this matter of suffering and be changed where our old man is made conformable unto His death.

One can know the Bible and not know God at all. The Devil is not an atheist and knows the Bible better than all of us. He can quote it, debate it, attack it, but cannot experience the life of the God of the Bible through the inception of faith. Knowing God is about the one taking this journey through the twists and turns in this journey of faith. The experimental witness of walking with God through loneliness, suffering, mountaintops, and others speaks of the one who is in active participation in this lifelong quest of the pursuit of God. Such are those who can come to times of ecstasies from their intimacy with Christ and declare "joy unspeakable and full of glory." Such do not need to work up happiness or have to go from one activity to another or be pandered to by "great" preachers but see the natural outflow of joy by the fruit of the Spirit. Those who are content to live on the sidelines get to heaven so as by fire.

Prayer

O God of heaven, thou who rulest all things well for in thy wisdom are we made. We bow in worship and adoration, for we desire thee and thee alone. Deliver us from the nearsightedness that makes us impatient and give up on the privilege to know thee. We covet after John, who lay at thy bosom on that momentous evening, desiring to hear from thee. We long to join the choir of angels and saints who have gone before us and are now enjoying thy presence unhindered. O that I may know Him, is our cry, turn us again, O God, and cause thy face to shine upon thy servant.

Day 18

Pilgrims to the Eternal Kingdom

Set your affection on things above, not on things on
the earth. For ye are dead, and your life is hid
with Christ in God. - Colossians 3:2-3

Close to the dawn of creation, Abraham was called and given a heart hunger for God that kept him to the very end. The enjoyment of God belongs to those who have turned away from Vanity Fair and have set their eyes and affections on things above. The Christian life is the greatest life, only to those who are spiritually minded, to the worldly-minded, it is a pretty miserable life with dos and don'ts, fearful of the whiplash that will fall on his back if he fails to obey. Those who vacillate between Christ and the world live with an unhealthy fear and bondage; they sadly miss out on the awesome privilege of being a pilgrim unto whom the world and its earthly goods have no binding cords that pull him down. Those who are heavenly-minded do the most earthly good. It is a known fact that the greatest movements to help the oppressed were done by those who were the most impacted by the glory of God and the responsibility that they saw to share that glory with others. William Booth freed the slums of England, William Carey helped end Sati, John Wesley's fight against Slavery, David Livingston's heart for Africa, John Paton reached Cannibals, Gladys Aylward saved Chinese orphans, and many others stand as witnesses. Such was the overwhelming cry of the Puritans who crossed the Atlantic by the Providence of God to establish one nation under God, with liberty and justice for all. Such overwhelming desire defines the pilgrim who is captivated by God's Kingdom, comes out to do the most good, and brings as many as will come to His eternal kingdom.

Seeking a city not made with hands has been the trademark of his journey, but he is not lost or has fanciful ideas, but knowing the reality of what he is looking for ploughs through doubts and embraces God with a heart full of faith. The nature of the Kingdom speaks to the value of his search. He is well aware of the things of this Earth that grow strangely dim and never last any sensible period of time. He knows that he could be called to follow the footsteps of the martyrs who have gone before him, but with steadfast faith, he presses into God, finding fulfillment in Him. And so, he ventures upon the God of the word who has promised him and looks for it as a costly pearl of great value.

To have the mind of a pilgrim needs more than just sentimental bursts of short-lived interest. Having known the fragility of life with its twists and turns, it prepares us to seek something more permanent. And this journey of faith is like the calm stream which has unfathomable depths. It is not the shallow shores that make the greatest disturbance that defines this man but rather a calm assurance that all is well. From such depths, one can see the face of death and sing; it is well with my soul. His sails have been set, the bridges have been burned, and there is no turning back.

Prayer

Dear Lord Jesus, we come to thee in the garb of Earth-mindedness in looking around to see what we can leave behind as a legacy of achievements. How shallow is our vision that is content with Earth's joys and fails to see the eternal kingdom that we ought to seek after. Help us as we live in this world, not to be off this world. And then may we rise up daily to drink from thy heavenly fountain and go on our earthly pilgrimage. Help us we pray to be doers of the word and not hearers only, deceiving our own selves.

The Goodness and Severity of God

*Teaching us that, denying ungodliness and worldly lusts,
we should live soberly, righteously, and godly,
in this present world - Titus 2:12*

It is the folly of man to take what suits his taste and conveniently ignore the rest. We sow our wild oats and hope for a harvest of wheat. The law of sowing and reaping has principles that are undeniable and cannot be changed. We wish to live like Demas and die like the apostle Paul. A man who is willing to give partial credence to the gospel is happy to think about the goodness of God and to proclaim it. It suits his ideology of God and sees Him as a great benefactor while having a sentimental attachment to a god of his making. Follow peace with all men is his cry, but he fails to continue to read the rest of the command that demands "and holiness, without which no man shall see the Lord." - Heb. 12:14. To him, God can only be consistent in such things that he favors as love, happiness, peace, goodness, etc. To relate to God as a God of wrath (Rom. 1:18), a God of judgment (Luke 12:5), an angry God (Psa. 7:11), the God who kills (Deut. 32:39), and so forth, he feels, is inconsistent with his view of God.

A God who condones evil and does not punish sin or fails to uphold the moral attributes of His nature in a sin-cursed world and in eternity is a monster. Sadly, the same man can look at the great evil that has been committed by men of the past and stand in judgment against them while excusing them in himself. Such is the heart of man that is desperately wicked, from which came such evil and debauchery that one may read in the pages of History. The rebellious subject who fails to relinquish his sword and submit to his Lord will never be accepted into the kingdom. The severity of God speaks of the rightness of God that flows from His nature as a holy God. The goodness of God, despite the intense consequences of sin and the final judgment, made a way of escape through the blood sacrifice of the Lord Jesus Christ by His own body. This defines the kindness of God to undeserved creatures. There is a rich man in hell today who cries for a drop of water being tormented in the flames of hell, who realizes this truth in its fullness. Where the goodness of God should have led him to repentance on Earth by the blessings that he received from God, he spurned and rejected it and is now faced with the severity of God for all of eternity.

Our brief time that we sojourn on this Earth is to have the proper balance of going to God in reverential fear, reflecting on the severity of God, and with worship and adoration bow before Him when reflecting upon the goodness of God that He has bestowed upon us by our redemption. Moses was told to take off his shoes, for he was on holy ground, and as we come to Him knowing the implication of who God is, it will be good for us to do the same while we lay prostrate before Him.

Prayer

Glorious Savior, eternal God to whom belongeth judgment, righteousness, and honor, we come before thee to rise above the clatter of human wisdom that hides thy face from us. We come in the merits of thy dear Son, asking thee to come among us as we desire to see thee in all thy beauty for the love wherewith thou hast loved us. I come as mortal flesh and enter into thy presence through the righteousness of Christ, desiring to know more of thee. I detest human pride that denies thy rightful place; instead, I come as a little child desiring all of thee. And then may I rise to know thee, the only true God, now and forever, Amen.

Day 20

The 'O' of the Thirsty Soul

Oh that thou wouldest rend the heavens, that thou
wouldest come down, that the mountains might
flow down at thy presence - Isaiah 64:1

The old Welsh divines called Revival as God visiting His garden. There is a great danger in praying for God's will while already knowing what to do, though under the guise of doing it for the glory of God. The true God of the Bible is unpredictable in His goings and comings, and the one thing that defined the early church is its unpredictability. The nature of the atmosphere of that church was its ability to change its environment with the power of the Spirit. "They turned the world upside down" was not the declaration of the church but the angry consternation of those who were opposed to it. The romance of the gospel is in the reality of the thirsty soul that finds, at times, calling out as a bride who has the yearnings towards her newlywed husband who has gone on a long journey. The sacred expression that one is brought to has the element of 'O' in it. Isaiah declares, Oh that thou wouldest rend the heavens (Isa. 64), Hannah groans in her barrenness, O Lord of hosts, and makes a vow (1 Sam. 1), the psalmist in despair cries out, Turn us again, O God (Psa. 80). The 'O' in Revival praying.

Such expressions are not the canned prayers of a well-known orator but the groaning of the inner man who has been thus brought to a state of despair. The man who speaks of the Christian life as all of hope and joy and fun has never entered into the sacred well that has become dry and cries out such groanings. He is not a man who can go along with convenient Christianity but feels that he will die young because of the heart pangs that he goes through. He does not evaluate where he is in the Christian life but rather finds himself in this place after years of getting to know God. He is no stranger to sacrifice or hardship but sees it as a small price to pay to the treasury of God while living this brief vapor of life.

Draw me nearer, nearer, blessed Lord, was the prayer of Fanny Crosby so wonderfully portrayed in that hymn. To rise to heights with God cannot be a momentary spark that dies in aborted prayers. William Cowper, in his moments of chronic depression, wrote, "Return, O holy Dove, return, sweet messenger of rest; I hate the sins that made Thee mourn, and drove Thee from my breast." But God, who is rich in mercy and loved us so, is well able to bring us to glorious heights by His grace and see the land of promise from the delectable mountaintops. To go on with God is the cry of the glorious witnesses who have gone before us and the angels who stand by our side, pointing the way to Mt. Zion. To those who are content to be spiritual pygmies and live in the lowlands, the air is damp, and their vision stunted while being earthbound. Their 'O' is directed to themselves in self-pity while complaining about the misery of life and die mumbling, "few and evil have the days of the years of my life been, and have not attained unto the days of the years of the life of my fathers in the days of their pilgrimage."

Prayer

O glorious King, our hands are feeble and our feet unsteady as we climb the mountain to get to thee. Come my soul, follow hard after Him, for He has promised to be faithful to have called us and also to do it. We rest on thee, and in thy name we go. We cast all of ourselves upon Him, this journey of God that knows no limits; the enjoyment of God that is inexhaustible for all of eternity.

Let All Mortal Flesh Keep Silence
Gerard Moultrie

Let all mortal flesh keep silence,
and with fear and trembling stand;
ponder nothing earthly minded,
for, with blessing in His hand,
Christ our God to earth descendeth,
our full homage to demand.

King of kings, yet born of Mary,
as of old on earth He stood,
Lord of lords, in human vesture,
in the body and the blood.
He will give to all the faithful
His own self for heav'nly food.

Rank on rank the host of heaven
spreads its vanguard on the way,
as the Light of light descendeth
from the realms of endless day,
that the pow'rs of hell may vanish
as the darkness clears away.

At His feet the six-winged seraph,
cherubim with sleepless eye,
veil their faces to the Presence,
as with ceaseless voice they cry,
"Alleluia, alleluia,
alleluia, Lord Most High!"

Day 21

Gird up now thy Loins

*Where wast thou when I laid the foundations of the
earth? declare, if thou hast understanding. - Job 38:4*

There has always been a constant struggle between the behavior of man and the advances that man has made that, at times, define his behavior. Though such transitions are normal and natural in the world around us, it is something that has been predicted by God in the time of Daniel around 539 BC that "knowledge shall be increased." - Dan. 12:4. The temptation is to come to the wrong conclusion about the need of man and present the wrong remedy which not only fails to solve the issue but creates a prejudice that brings doubt to the validity of God's remedy. In the time of Darwin, man embraced his "deliverance" from God and thought he came from lower primates; during the Industrial Revolution, man embraced his advancements and felt enlightened about his strength; in the atomic age, man felt he was unstoppable and science, that he defined, had the answers; in the dawn of the AI (Artificial Intelligence) revolution, man feels he has entered into the realm of infinite possibilities and has become like a god. Yet, the message from the time of Adam has been that the fundamental problem of man is not in his environment or surroundings, rather, it is much deeper in his heart that he is dead in trespasses and sins.

The remedy of man has not changed, for it deals with the nature of man. Only by God can he be changed. From one who has a disposition towards sin to one who is changed to have a disposition towards holiness, given from the One who has imparted of His own nature and creates in him a new heart. In the meanwhile, man is happy to have religion, atheism, entertainment, relationships, and a myriad of others to hide behind his folly. Such is the depravity of man, who cannot receive the things of the Spirit of God and, by his own wisdom, cannot know God. In the end, man will be confounded and face a holy God who will bring him into account for all that he has done in rejecting God, the God who so loved him.

The heart yearning for the one who has been freed from this vicious cycle of ignorance to serve the living God, his Creator, realizes that the residue of unbelief can linger in the heart when endeavoring to take this journey with God. To foster a deep longing for God, one must put away all doubts of the trustworthiness of God and cast oneself unto the unseen One who is able to bring us from faith to faith. To the arrogant man who is equipped with hard questions about God for entrapment and revealing his own ignorance, the answer comes from an unlikely source, the response of a prodigal in the pigpen "when he came to himself," to arise and go to where the answers are, the God of the Universe through the lowly Jesus. God calls to those content in apathy to "Gird up now thy loins like a man; for I will demand of thee, and answer thou me" - Job 38:3. The excuses for not seeking after God will then vanish, and we will face the One unto whom we will have to give an answer.

Prayer

Oh Lord, how I tremble at the thought of man's folly and wretched unbelief, how arrogant is he to stand in judgment of the One who has given him life and holds his breath in His hands? He whose beat of the heart is not guaranteed raises up his fist against the Almighty. Yet, Lord, I come in humble desire to gird up my loins and seek after thee earnestly with all my heart. Instill in me thy desire to run hard after thee that I may know thee and love thee with all my heart, might, mind, and strength, now and forever. This is my humble prayer.

Day 22

The Eternal Word of the word

In the beginning God - Genesis 1:1

The greatness of God does not only consist of His majesty revealed in creation, miracles that He performed, and so forth, it is also in the fact that God gave us His word and preserved it from generation to generation. The infallibility and inerrancy of Scripture is not about a man's claim to manipulate the masses, but rather, it is an obvious outcome when we realize that all Scripture is given by inspiration of God, in other words, "God-breathed." When John declared, "In the beginning was the Word, and the Word was with God, and the Word was God." - John 1:1, he was not making a statement for us to wrestle with. He was indeed stating a fact that is true for all eternity that Christ always was, is, and will be. The birth of Christ, his incarnation upon Earth, is not the beginning of Christ but rather the continuance of His preexistence, the glory He shared with His Father, being co-equal with God, made manifest among us.

Too many theologians, in their folly and foolishness, have made it their lifelong ambition to make Christ a little less than God. In that declaration to Phillip, "he that hath seen me hath seen the Father" (John 14:9), God, who is a Spirit where no man can see and live, has taken on human flesh while in no way abdicating His Godhood. The tragedy of man choosing portions of the Scripture that fit with his conception of God will bring about his own destruction. There is one God who gave us one word written through 40 penmen, giving one message to all of mankind for all time, the completed Canon of Scripture in its sixty-six books. The accursed of God who preaches another gospel, in essence, another christ, may have a multitude of followers, but it will never stand in the bar of God on judgment day. The revelation of the Word from the word is the exclusive work of the precious Holy Spirit of God, the Person. The one who wrote the book is the One who can effectively expound the book. And yet the warning is there to try the spirits whether they be of God. There's only one standard of truth from the God who deals with absolutes, and it is the infallible word of God, all of it. The milk and meat for the thirsty soul.

The searching heart that desires communion with Christ, as in the days of Christ upon the Earth, must be careful not to look for an experience that is not warranted by the Scriptures. God will never contradict what He has said, and one must always seek the truth by the Spirit through the word. Only truth can lead us to the revelation of God in experiential witness and bring us onward to adoration and worship. The deepening of faith, knowledge of the holy, and doctrine are made possible to those who lay prostrate before Him as they meditate on the word of God. The entrance of thy word giveth light, and the Spirit of God will give life to that light, where Christ is all the more lovely to the beholding eye. To the academic agnostic, the Bible is a closed book, but to the humble child of God, he can testify that man shall not live by bread alone but by every word that proceedeth out of the mouth of God.

Prayer

Eternal God who cannot be contained by the heavens, I come as a little child who is overwhelmed by thy greatness and the eternal truths that have been given to us through the pages of thy eternal word. Help us, O God, for our eyes are dim from beholding earthly things. May the preciousness of thy word and its reality lift us to higher ground. May thy truth set us free from the shackles of doubt that we may rise in faith and meet our God.

Everything Stems from God's Nature

*But as he which hath called you is holy, so be ye holy
in all manner of conversation; Because it is written,
Be ye holy; for I am holy. - 1 Peter 1:15-16*

Certain truths are so fundamental in nature that they can be detrimental if seen in the wrong way. In a world that constantly deals with subjective ideas that undermine absolute truth, the great need we have before us is to ensure that we stand on solid ground. The ignoramus critique of the Bible, in his pride, sits on his pedestal, placing himself as a judge against God, whose name is Holy. God's nature is holy, which cannot be comprehended in its full essence while we are in this world. By grace, are ye saved is the only possible explanation when realizing the holiness of God, who hates iniquity and condemns the sinner to the lake of fire for all eternity. The seraphims could not look upon him when they cried out, "Holy, holy, holy, is the Lord of hosts" - Isa. 6:3. They were declaring the nature of God. God always acts in accordance with His nature, and He cannot contradict Himself.

To the arrogant critic, God's judgments may seem incompatible with his definition of a God of love. The judgment of God that fell upon the Canaanites, as well as upon His own people, speaks to the nature of God no matter who they were. Unless we are convinced of the reality that God always works in consistent with His holiness and all His actions stem from that, God will seem like a tyrant. We don't dictate the rules; God does, and He has, as our Maker, every right to demand His way. While the casual reader of the Scriptures can falsely see the God of the Old Testament as a bully, the eternal truth of God remains that God is holy, and there is no unrighteousness in Him. The terror of those who exclaimed for the rocks to fall upon them rather than face the wrath of the Lamb (Rev. 6:16) speaks to the reality of this truth that God judges sin. The tragedy of sin of what it portrays as "acceptable reality" has been corrupted to such a point where the essence of truth is hidden, and evil is called good.

To meditate upon God as the God of love and ignore, to our own detriment, the God of justice is to be inconsistent with the Scriptures and cause shipwreck to our faith. Our responsibility is to take the truth in its entirety and bow in worship, having the proper fear of God. Isaiah's problem was not on the nature of God but rather on his own relation to the revelation of that nature, which caused him to cry out, "Woe is me!" The gentle Jesus, meek and mild, who is now glorified as Lord and Christ, while He shows compassion to the trembling sinner, will be a terror to His enemies. Though He is touched by the feelings of our infirmities, the wicked shall be turned into hell, and all the nations that forget God.

Prayer

Holy Father, to thee, belongeth truth and to us confusion. We tremble at the thought of thy holiness and approach thee through the covering of the blood of thy dear Son. Though we cry, depart from me, Lord, for I am a sinful man, we run towards thee, for in thee is life eternal. Thy witness bear in our hearts by thy Spirit that we are thine and thine alone, and may thy word bring us comfort in this truth that we cry, Abba, Father. With offerings of praise for the forgiveness of our sins, we come with grateful hearts for the privilege to be partakers of thy holiness.

Day 24

The Burnings of God

Who among us shall dwell with the devouring
fire? who among us shall dwell with
everlasting burnings? - Isaiah 33:14

God works from eternity to eternity; unbound by time, matter, and space, He is continually worshiped and inhabits the praises of His people, dwelling in the light which no man can approach unto (1 Tim. 6:16). When we think about the sights of heaven, a flood of thoughts occupies our mind as we look at the Scriptures and realize the tremendous imagery that is given of what the prophets saw in their revelation of God. Seeing the glorified Christ, John speaks of the Apocalypse with words that are hard to comprehend in human understanding. Isaiah, standing in that place of holiness before the throne of God, cries, "Woe is me!" Job going through great sorrow and suffering when confronted with the Almighty cries, "Behold, I am vile; what shall I answer thee? I will lay mine hand upon my mouth." We are given a brief glimpse of one imagery that seems to bring us to a deeper understanding of God's transcendent dwelling when Isaiah asks the rhetorical question, "who among us shall dwell with everlasting burnings?"

The metal being fashioned is put in a furnace and beaten to conform to the image of the desire of the blacksmith. It learns to stay in the fire until it is red-hot and malleable. The burnings of God speak of the tremendous void that man is subject to because of the Fall, and which can only be filled by God. Such was the burnings of the men from Emmaus who found the resurrected Christ where they exclaimed, "Did not our heart burn within us, while he talked with us by the way, and while he opened to us the scriptures?" - Luke 24:32. The living God dwelling among sinful men gives hope to the child of God to seek after Him until He is found and to be in the place of dwelling among the burnings of God.

The three Hebrew children met the pre-incarnate Christ in the burnings, and they were able to enjoy the presence of God unscathed by the fire or its power over them. God, who is rich in mercy and desirous for His children to experience Him, at times, brings us to the place of burnings that can cause us to know His cleansing power. He brings us to the place of holy ground to meet Him by the burning bush to hear from Him and to love and worship him. The fellowship that Christ enjoyed with His Father was such that the glory of the kingdoms of this world that Satan tempted Him with would have been as refuse when compared to His place in the bosom of His Father. In the same way, the desire of the heart fulfilled is such that he is filled with the Spirit of God and gets to enjoy the fellowship of God, where all the world would be as dung when compared to such times of refreshing.

Prayer

Lord God, our gracious Savior who met those disciples on the road to Emmaus, come and break thou the Bread of heaven and feed us. Teach us thy way as we desire thee. May our hearts burn for the knowledge of thee which affects our passion for thee, and with one voice, we lift up our hearts in worship to thee. And may we go with our hearts carrying such burnings to a lost and dying world that has no hope beyond the grave and declare, Behold the Lamb of God, which taketh away the sin of the world. Set our hearts on fire for thy great name's sake.

Day 25

The Jealousy of God

For thou shalt worship no other god: for the Lord, whose
name is Jealous, is a jealous God: - Exodus 34:14

There are some things we feel are not consistent with the nature of God, such is the deception of our hearts when considering the jealousy of God. Jealousy has the picture of desiring something that is not ours or as being related to covetousness. But a husband who is jealous because of an unfaithful wife is not only natural, but one would fundamentally question his character if he behaved on the contrary. God's picture of jealousy in Hosea speaks of the intermingling of human emotions, which gives us a rare glimpse into the heart of God. The heart-wrenching sight of a man seeing his wife play the harlot, going after her in love to bring her back and speak words of love and kindness, is imagery that is hard to grasp when thinking about God Almighty dealing with His children.

The danger we have which brings God to our level must be avoided. Instead, the inward awe and solemnity that we ought to have towards God for His covering over us is the right response. The place of Moses as an intercessor speaks to this nature of God, who stayed the hand of God from certain judgment upon the people of Israel who had gone after the golden calf. There are sacred texts given about God that we can go no further from that which has been given. Texts such as "his soul grieved for the misery of Israel" - Judg. 10:16 and "mine heart is turned within me, my repentings are kindled together" - Hos. 11:8. Such expressions from God, who does not change, should not cause us to make foolish assumptions, as the Universalist does, but to get to know this God.

Where do we go from here? Are we in a position to liken God to one of us? That would be preposterous. God does everything based on His nature of holiness. Even in the instances that He is said to have repented, it is from holiness to holiness. We, on the other hand, repent from sinfulness. This response of God should cause both awe and godly fear. Awe, that God, who has begotten us and positioned us as the bride of Christ, is jealous over us. Such knowledge cautions us to keep ourselves unspotted from this world. "And every man that hath this hope in him purifieth himself" - 1 John 3:3, and have a godly fear lest we grieve His heart of love towards us. The chaste bride keeps herself pure, as this goes both ways. The man who desires to cultivate a deep thirst for God will constantly look to the One whom he is in love with, grieved at the reproach that is on His name, and does not care what others think of him. He is jealous that He must be glorified even at the expense of his own humiliation. He goes unto Him without the camp, bearing His reproach. The portrayal of such deep affection is displayed in "Let him kiss me with the kisses of his mouth: for thy love is better than wine" - Song. 1:2. The interplay in the Song of Solomon speaks of God-initiated redemptive love and my response in reciprocal love to Him, the enjoyment of each other in a sacred context through using natural and human imagery.

Prayer

Jesus, lover of my soul, we come to thee and share in thy love that thou hast shed abroad in our hearts. Thy love displayed on Calvary rises in declaring its witness of thy jealous espousal of us, thy children. Be still my soul and gaze upon Him, the joy of heaven. Let love rise from within to cleave to Him and whisper songs of love to thy Beloved. I come to thee in seasons of winter, to yearn and seek after thee that I may once again whisper, I am my Beloved's, and my Beloved is mine.

The God of Creation

The heavens declare the glory of God; and the
firmament sheweth his handywork. - Psalm 19:1

There's an old saying by Samuel Taylor Coleridge that states that "Water cannot rise higher than its source, neither can human reason." The declaration of God in creation shows the magnitude of God in His greatness to bring everything we see into existence in six literal days over six thousand years ago. Elijah boldly declared, "the God that answereth by fire, let him be God." - 1 Kings 18:24. In this modern age of advancement, where man seems to think he has the upper hand, he is nevertheless extremely limited in his knowledge and understanding. The vastness of space, the impossibility of physical constraints that he cannot overcome, the motives of others that he struggles to understand, the results of a world in chaos that he tries to imagine that he has an answer for, and many more speak of the smallness of man and the greatness of God who said, "Let there be light: and there was light" - Gen. 1:3. The problem is not that man has no evidence for God rather the problem is that he has no answer to why he is fearfully and wonderfully made apart from God. And what he tries to put together to quench his void falls painfully short.

The heavens declare the glory of God. He fills the heart that is in tune with the Almighty, who is willing to receive and enjoy what God has done. God asks the rhetorical question, "Behold, I am the Lord, the God of all flesh: is there any thing too hard for me?" - Jer. 32:27. To those struggling in faith, seeing the unknownness of tomorrow, we must look at God's creation and its impeccable order and ask the question: If I don't doubt that the sun will rise tomorrow, why should I doubt the God who made the sun and its cycles, and upholds them? Sadly, the natural man receiveth not the things of the Spirit of God for they are foolishness unto him, neither can he know them, because they are spiritually discerned, but we who have been awakened, redeemed, cleansed, and changed should yearn to know this God who has done all things well.

Yet, there is something far greater. The greatness of redemption supersedes the majesty of creation. It is the impossibility of a holy God and the sinful man being able to commune together. But come together they may because of the righteousness of Christ. "that they might know thee the only true God, and Jesus Christ" was Christ's desire. The Spirit that birthed Christ in the womb of the virgin Mary is the same Spirit that births a man who has been awakened to his need and is born into the kingdom of God. Such is the beauty of the work of grace that multitudes rise up, from wise men to ignoramuses, from humble men to kings, from super intellectuals to simpletons, from the poor to the rich, they rise from all nations and tribes and declare, "we thank thee, and praise thy glorious name" - 1 Chr. 29:13.

Prayer

Glorious Creator, I stand in awe of thy work though tainted by the Fall. O wretched man, how far hast thou fallen from grace? Once created in purity but now content to grovel in darkness. How desirous is sin the enemy of your soul, darkened without light; An ally of the flesh, content to spend the vapor of time in perpetual blindness. Bent to sin and desiring pleasure for a season while spurning eternity. In utter blindness with no light within, having the heart entwined to wickedness, May God grant thee favor to send thee light; for all goodness comes from thee, O God.

Day 27

When Heaven Draws Near

*Repent ye therefore, and be converted, that your sins may
be blotted out, when the times of refreshing shall come
from the presence of the Lord. - Acts 3:19*

The fundamental nature of Christianity that makes it different than all other so-called religions of this world is the fact of God in the midst of His people. The living and only true God who made the heavens and the earth showed Himself by His visible, manifest presence when the Shekinah glory came down and filled that Tabernacle in the barren plains of the desert. In the same essence, the presence was lifted many times when sin entered the camp, and the people were left with a form of religion. Ichabod was not only declaring the absence of God but also the frown of His displeasure. The god who is always sympathetic to his people, though they commit sin and do not punish them, is not the God of the Bible. The spotted history of Israel speaks of the God who rescued them with a great victory but turned around and punished and scattered them because of their evil, which is something that we have to reckon with.

To think of such action as an Old Testament event and not necessarily in the new covenant of grace is to deny the truth of Scripture and declare that we worship two gods who are diametrically opposed to each other. The same judgment of God can be seen in the life of the early church with the death of Ananias and Sapphira (Acts 5:1-11), Paul giving the believer over to Satan for the destruction of the flesh (1 Cor. 5:5), etc. When the church has found herself in her greatest moments of despair and barrenness, by a sudden and sovereign act of mercy, God intervened and poured out His Spirit upon His people where heaven draws nigh of what we call Revival. This is not something that can be scheduled, organized, advertised, or done by any human agent who can bring it about. It is something God does, though He uses human instruments for such a work.

Such times of refreshing are irritable to the carnal man who is comfortable in his apathy and is quite willing to live in his well-organized religion and say his prayers. But to the soul that has been touched by a longing for God, who is not content with the status quo, he will be looked at by the rest as a fanatic and as one who is irrelevant to modern society. But such souls are the hope of the church where God can lay a burden as He prepares such people to be able to receive such moves of God and be a channel where the waters flow. A flood of blessings to all around them. Such men are refined in the crucible of God's furnace until they are ready to be brought forth, to stand in the gap between a dying church and an angry God. These are those whose lungs have been filled with the breath of heaven and have walked the long, lonely road of jagged mountain tops in communion with God. Such radical sacrifices are needed for our day. May God break through and rend the heavens and come down. An eruption of Divine disorder.

Prayer

God of heaven and earth, I have heard thy voice and was afraid, make thy desires known in this day of wretched shallowness. Hear us, O God, hear us and cause thy face to shine upon us. Prepare thy servant as I long after thee, hungering and thirsting after thee. May the glory be thine and thine alone forever and ever, Amen.

Day 28

Dwelling place of God

That I may know him - Philippians 3:10

The pages of holy writ from Genesis to Revelation speak of the common theme of God's redemption of man through Jesus Christ, the author and finisher of our faith. The eternal question of the angels who are unable to comprehend declares, "can God indeed dwell among men?" The impossibility of reconciliation between a holy God and sinful man is not a theme for a theological debate; instead, it is a reality of the impossibility of mortal man being able to reach out to an immortal God. Man had his dwelling among God in the garden of Eden, where God met him in the cool of the day and blessed the marriage union of Adam and Eve, one man and one woman for life. They lost their privilege because of sin, being chased out and having their dwelling in the dry and arid land of thorns and thistles, the ground cursed, to sweat and toil and labor for unfruitful harvest.

From this bleak picture, we ask ourselves to consider if God can indeed dwell with man. Jacob found this on his way to Padanaram, on that dream of the ladder to heaven, he woke up, and he was afraid because the Lord was in that place. He declared, "How dreadful is this place! this is none other but the house of God, and this is the gate of heaven" - Gen. 28:17. Moses standing by the burning bush was afraid to look upon God (Exo. 3:6), Joshua standing at the beginning of the conquest of Canaan bowed to the ground when confronted by the pre-incarnate Christ having His sword drawn (Jos. 5:13-15), John who lay on the bosom of Christ fell at His feet as dead when he saw Him in glory (Rev. 1:17). Such scenes of encounters with God speak of the grand and solemn privilege such men have had to experience the manifest presence of God and Christ. For the man who has his eyes on this world, such experiences soon fade away and seem trivial when compared to his captivation of fleeting pleasures, that are worthless.

Yet we are not left to our imagination; instead, we are lifted up to God's declaration of His dwelling place. "For thus saith the high and lofty One that inhabiteth eternity, whose name is Holy; I dwell in the high and holy place, with him also that is of a contrite and humble spirit, to revive the spirit of the humble, and to revive the heart of the contrite ones." - Isa. 57:15. Thus, the dwelling place of God came into the heart of that woman who showed adoration and worship when she broke the alabaster box, with tears washed His feet, with her hair wiped it, kissed them in love, and lavished freely the ointment upon them. Glory divine, wonderful Savior who comes and dwells in the heart of man. Henry Scougal depicts it well when he titled his book "The Life of God in the Soul of Man." The proper response of those overwhelmed by such grace will be to proclaim, thanks be to God for His unspeakable gift (2 Cor. 9:15).

Prayer

Dear Lord, we are unable to adequately represent how our hearts feel as we rise and offer our worship to thee. We realize the curse of words, for it falls short of the beauty and glory of our heavenly King, unable to express using earthly form. I come to thee for thou hast desired me and entwined thy joy in the fulfillment of our union with thee; and my joy I find in thee. We praise thee, O God, glorify thy name now and forever, Amen.

Day 29

Entering into His Throne Room

Enter into his gates with thanksgiving, and into his
courts with praise: be thankful unto him,
and bless his name. - Psalm 100:4

The Old Testament picture of the Tabernacle was a visible testimony of God's presence among the people of God. When the fire of the Lord filled the holy of holies, it was declared miles away that God lived here. To enter into such a place was to be done with great reverence, realizing the deep implications of a mortal man meeting God. Yet Moses, Aaron, and others did not see the finality of Christ's earth-rending call, "it is finished." Oh, praise the Lord, the work is done, what the first Adam could not do the final Adam has accomplished, "Alleluia; Salvation, and glory, and honour, and power, unto the Lord our God" - Rev. 19:1. Such was the implication of this momentous event that it rent the rocks and made creation groan with earthquakes, so much so that the centurion declared, "Truly this was the Son of God" - Mat. 27:54. Justice has been satisfied, and the veil of the temple rent in twain from the top to the bottom.

The solemn act of Christ to reconcile man was so high a cost, and Christ bearing His wounds for all of eternity would be a sight that cannot be expressed. It was by His own blood that He entered once into the holy place, having obtained eternal redemption for us. We now have access to the holy of holies through our great High Priest, Jesus Christ. God now declares that we can enter boldly unto the throne of grace, that we may obtain mercy, and find grace to help in time of need (Heb. 4:16). This boldness is not about the arrogance that a spoiled child displays when he wants his way. Instead, it is the confidence of our position in Christ that we dared to call Him "Our Father." Do it in remembrance of me was the command of Christ, and we partake in a solemn assembly of remembering God's great sacrifice for us, the Passover Lamb of God. The implication of this can never be fully understood, and there is a danger of being able to explain it away as an act of technicality in a mechanical fashion. Partaking of the Lord's supper must bring us to the place of speechless adoration of the Lamb at Calvary. Let us approach with reverential fear and thanksgiving.

As we come to such truths of the death of Christ and His glorious resurrection, we are reminded of Christ's priestly prayer that we may be One in Him and share the glories of heaven, enjoying God forever. Such was the great work of God that Christ went further to call us to a more intimate love relationship that is similitude of a bride and his groom. As we continue in this earthly journey, He has called us His friends, for He has made known unto us His love and has revealed the Father in human flesh in Himself, God incarnate. Anthropomorphism realized. Friendship with God should cause us to bow down in worship to thank Him, and as He lifts up our heads, we go with hearts full of love towards Him.

Prayer

Dear Lord Jesus, for centuries, a multitude of people have sung praises to thy name. I thank thee for thy love to come among us. Wonderful, Counselor, Almighty God, Everlasting Father, the Prince of Peace. We enter into the outer court in preparation to meet thee; we enter into the holy place with earnest expectation, having the assurance of the covering of the blood of Christ upon us; and we enter in awe and reverential godly fear into the holy of holies and behold thee and experience thy presence. Selah.

Day 30

Be Still and Know

Take my yoke upon you, and learn of me; for I am
meek and lowly in heart: and ye shall find
rest unto your souls. - Mathew 11:29

The busyness of life demands man's attention. To come to the end of a day and feel like nothing has been accomplished has been the norm many a time. To take the yoke of Christ is not the path of ease, but to know that the yoke was never meant to be pulled alone is comforting. When Abram fell into a deep sleep, a horror of darkness fell upon him; he was in a place of stillness where God was able to speak. In our generation, we look to technology to find ways to reduce our downward spin, but sadly, we find that our day has become even more busy and time an elusive master. Being still has a two-pronged meaning. One, of being still to see God move on our behalf, such as Moses on his face before God at the Red Sea. But it is also addressed to His enemies to be still, to acknowledge God.

Society has made us into a fast-food culture and an impatient people. It spoiled us to get things immediately, and we got annoyed at someone who wanted to talk instead of serving our table. The impatient man has no time for deep and consequential reading and meditation. Instead, it is the man who has disciplined himself to be still who can take a chaotic environment and retire into the cloister of his heart and meet God there, in stillness. God's declaration, "Be still, and know that I am God" (Psa. 46:10) stands as a silent testimony for any trembling heart to hear and heed the call. The desire to plunge deep into God can come in any circumstance. D.L. Moody was walking down Wall Street in New York when the Spirit of God was poured out upon him, and he was endued with power from on high. Those who have experienced outpourings of the Spirit of God can testify of times when the whole audience was stilled and silence prevailed. Those present dared not to disturb His presence, which permeated and probed each individual. They, in a sense, tip-toed when leaving the Sanctuary, aware of this stillness, and felt it when they came close to the place.

To the proud man fighting against God, God declares, "I am God, and there is none else." Pharoah, who thought he had great power, came to the end of himself and could hear, "Be still, and know that I am God: I will be exalted among the heathen, I will be exalted in the earth." - Psa. 46:10. This matter of being still to the man who vainly opposes God, and (to him) God is declaring: be still, give up your position, lay down your weapons, and acknowledge me. For the Christian, this is not about being idle. It is one of the hardest things to do, to be still. It is an active submission while waiting on God, as Elijah did when he wrapped his face in his mantle upon hearing the still, small voice. Only in stillness is the heart calmed and made attentive to hear, and still waters run deep, which can receive large ships. The hymn puts it well, "Be still, my soul; the Lord is on thy side." The nearness of God, my reason be.

Prayer

Lord, we hush our hearts to hear thy voice and follow thee, desiring to be by thy side. The hour is late, and we cannot afford to be dulled by the voices of this world, where we don't recognize thy still small voice. Speak, Lord; for thy servant heareth, said Samuel in the stillness of the night. I come desiring as a little child and say, Speak Lord, ye who calmed the storms in the sea of Galilee saying peace be still, calm my storm that I may sense thy tug to forsake the voices that cry for my attention and follow only thee.

Day 31

Whosoever will may Come and Drink

But what saith it? The word is nigh thee, even in
thy mouth, and in thy heart: that is, the word of
faith, which we preach - Romans 10:8

The greatness of a statement is measured by the largeness of the person who says it. As we have begun this lifelong enjoyment of God, the path ahead of us seems bleak with twists and turns, and we wonder if we will be able to continue on without some external stimulus. The secret of the man who goes on with God is in his acknowledgment of his barrenness, the experiential knowledge of the Holy Spirit, the path of prayer, the word of God, acquainting oneself with historic revivals and lives of saints of the past, and the intentional actions taken to keep the fiery burnings on a day-to-day basis. Such work needs discipline, and those who lag behind find it hard and give up. "Watch ye, stand fast in the faith, quit you like men, be strong" - 1 Cor. 16:13, and to do it with charity (v14) is just as much a command as is a method for treading through this journey of knowing God. "the kingdom of heaven suffereth violence, and the violent take it by force" - Mat. 11:12. Yet the warning is that this knowledge is for the humble of heart, and the man who reasons within himself on the greatness of his knowing is treading on dangerous grounds. Pride was the fall of Lucifer, and the warning remains as a testimony throughout eternity for all to see. God resisteth the proud, and giveth grace to the humble.

The call is for all who desire to come and drink the water of life freely (Rev. 22:17). The man who feels his own inadequacy and smallness is called to the banquet just as much as the one who is full of faith and of the Holy Ghost. Wisdom crieth in the streets for all to hear (Prov. 1:20), yet man is deaf to the words of life and is distracted by the noise of his mundane nearsightedness. The folly of man to ignore God's call will be his greatest terror on what he could have been, and the path of the man of the world is strewed with the wreckage of wasted endeavors. Man was created for greatness, and the humble soul embraces the journey ahead and ploughs through the harsh winter so he may reach the golden shores where he can enjoy the sunshine of heaven, where God dwells. In beholding His beauty, he is content to have gone through and paid the price to meet it.

Cast off your earthly garments and join the throng of those who have gone before us and embrace the God who came to seek and save that which was lost. Delight in the Lord, and He shall give thee the desires of thine heart (Psa. 37:4), this is the promise. God does not have double standards. There have been those who have gone before us through rivers of blood to capture the prize, and He will not relinquish that cost to those who are unwilling to walk in His prescribed pathway. Those who have met God beckon us to follow on and live in the perpetual vision of the most high God.

Prayer

Oh Lord, thou art God, and I come to thee on my knees, with hands lifted and hearts stilled as I ponder the days ahead, to continue on and trust thy care to bring me through day by day. Then will I live in thy love experienced, and though there may be days of sorrow, I long to see the grand unveiling of thy glory revealed and thy cause fulfilled. I desire a continual feast at thy table until that day when I shall see thee face to face. To thee belongeth glory, power, and honor, forever and ever world without end. Amen.

Be Thou My Vision
Dallán Forgaill

Be Thou my Vision, O Lord of my heart;
be all else but naught to me, save that Thou art;
be Thou my best thought in the day and the night,
both waking and sleeping, Thy presence my light.

Be Thou my Wisdom, be Thou my true Word;
be Thou ever with me and I with Thee, Lord;
be Thou my great Father, and I Thy true son,
be Thou in me dwelling, and I with Thee one.

Riches I heed not, nor man's empty praise,
be Thou mine inheritance, now and always;
be Thou and Thou only the first in my heart,
O High King of heaven, my Treasure Thou art.

High King of heaven, Thou heaven's bright Sun,
O grant me its joys, after vict'ry is won;
Great Heart of my own heart, whatever befall,
still be Thou my Vision, O Ruler of all.

public domain

About the Author

Jabez Abraham is the founder and president of Desiring Revival Ministries, an organization dedicated to fostering a deep thirst for God and making Christ known to all generations and nations (Habakkuk 2:14).

Soli Deo Gloria